Bear
Grylls

BEAR GRYLLS

ADVENTURE ANNUAL 2020

Conceived by Bonnier Books UK in partnership
with Bear Grylls Ventures

Produced by Bonnier Books UK

Suite 3.08 The Plaza, 535 Kings Road,
London SW10 0SZ, UK

© 2019 Bonnier Books UK

Design: Angela Ball, David Ball

Editorial: Claudia Martin, Susie Rae, Laura Pollard

Illustrations: Julian Baker, Bernard Chau, Peter Bull Studios

2 4 6 8 10 9 7 5 3 1

ISBN: 9781786961211

Disclaimer

Bonnier Books UK and Bear Grylls take pride in doing our best to get the facts right in putting
together the information in this book, but occasionally something slips past our beady eyes.
Therefore we make no warranties about the accuracy or completeness of the information
in the book, and to the maximum extent permitted, we disclaim all liability.
Wherever possible, we will endeavour to correct any errors of fact at reprint.

Kids – If you want to try any of the activities in this book, please ask your parents first!
Parents – All outdoor activities carry some degree of risk and we recommend that anyone participating
in these activities be aware of the risks involved and seek professional instruction and guidance.
None of the health/medical information in this book is intended as a substitute for professional
medical advice; always seek the advice of a qualified practitioner.

BEAR GRYLLS

ADVENTURE ANNUAL 2020

CONTENTS

We live on an amazing planet with so much to see, from towering mountains to deep, dark oceans. Since I was a child, I have always felt the pull of the wild. I've been lucky enough to have had the opportunity to go on many incredible adventures in some fantastic parts of the world, often to very remote places where only a few human beings have ever ventured before. Whether you are planning your own expedition or just settling down for a bedtime read, turn the page to find out how to survive in some of the world's most extreme environments. Along the way, you can do puzzles, learn about extraordinary animals, and find out about brave explorers. Enjoy the adventure!

Bear

HOW TO USE THIS BOOK

There are lots of facts and activities in this book, from vital survival skills to word searches. Check the symbol (see below) at the top left of each page, then decide whether you're in the mood for building your skills or learning some facts to amaze your friends! You will find the answers to the puzzles on page 72.

SYMBOL KEY

 ALL ABOUT

Discover some fascinating animals and how they survive in baking deserts or icy seas.

 **HABITAT**

Here's where you can learn key facts about demanding habitats so you will be prepared for anything.

 AMAZING ADVENTURES

Read the tales of adventurers (including me!) who have risked their lives to discover the world.

 SURVIVAL SKILLS

Brush up your skills before you head into the wild – learn how to light a fire, read a map, and forecast the weather!

 GET CREATIVE

Grab your pencil case and try some tricky puzzles, creative colouring, and fiendish investigations.

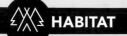

MOUNTAINS

◄ Mountains push any adventurer to their limits!

Mountains are one of the most demanding habitats, for animals, plants – and human adventurers! Even the most experienced mountain climbers are at risk from avalanches, hidden crevasses, freezing temperatures, and high altitudes. It is vital to train and prepare before even setting foot on a mountain.

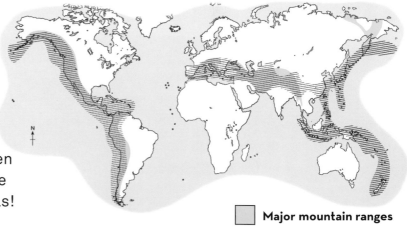

▼ Nothing can beat the rush you get when, after hours, days, or even months, of hard work, you finally reach the summit of a mountain!

WHAT IS A MOUNTAIN?

Mountains are made by the pressing together of the giant plates of rock that form the Earth's surface. Over millions of years, rock is forced up into folds and ridges. What's the difference between a hill and a mountain? Mountains are generally taller and steeper than hills!

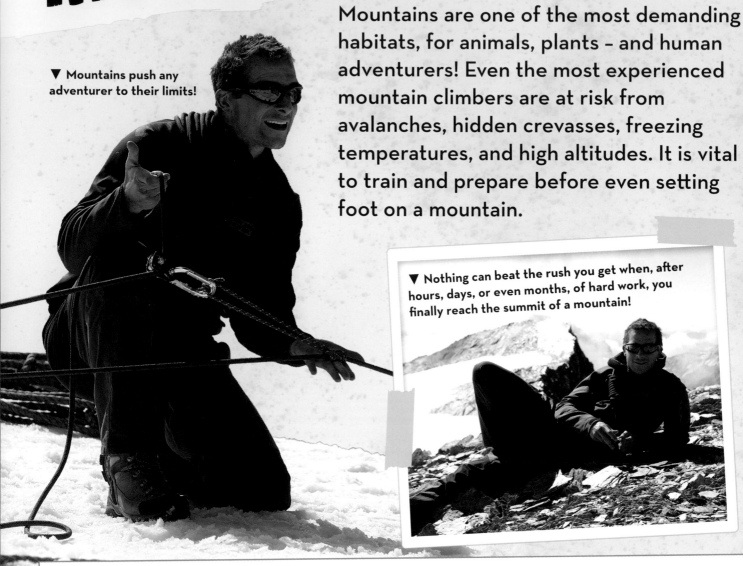

N

Major mountain ranges

MOUNTAIN SPORTS

There is a huge variety of fun sports and activities you can do in the mountains:

Hang gliding

This is an extreme sport where you are launched off a hill, attached to a giant, stringless kite called a hang glider. It is kept in the air with the help of warm air rising in columns called thermals.

Skiing

Skiing is not just a sport – it can also be a useful way of travelling around on snow. Originally done on wooden skis, people have been skiing for thousands of years.

Mountain biking

Mountain biking involves riding specially designed bikes off road. It's important to watch out for other people, and make sure you have permission to cycle in the area.

Rock climbing

You can climb up, down, and even across natural rocks. It's a lot of fun, and is a fantastic workout for your entire body! There are competitions where people will race across the rocks, trying to complete the course first, without falling.

⚠ DANGER: AVALANCHE!

An avalanche is a sudden, rapid flow of snow down a slope, often caused just by the weight of fallen snow. Remember these tips if you are ever caught in an avalanche:

❶ Try to escape to the side of an avalanche.

❷ If you are buried, spit out a bit of saliva as it will run downwards and help you work out which way is up.

❸ Before the snow stops moving, cup your hand in front of your face to create an airspace.

❹ If you are near the surface, try to get an arm or leg out to show others where you are.

dig an airspace in front of your face

KNOTS

Whether you're climbing Everest, camping in the foothills, or just out and about, knot tying is a vital skill... and a lot of fun! Why not try your hand at some of these clever knots?

FIGURE-OF-EIGHT LOOP

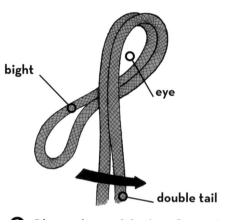

bight

eye

double tail

❶ Place a looped 'bight' of rope behind the double 'tail' of the rope.

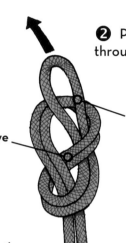

❷ Push the bight up through the original 'eye'.

bight goes through the eye of the rope

eye

❸ The finished knot should look a little like the number 8.

THREADED FIGURE-OF-EIGHT

❶ This knot allows you to attach yourself to a climbing harness. Start by tying a loose figure-of-eight knot, leaving a long tail. Thread the tail through the harness, then start threading it back through the top of the figure-of-eight.

harness

tail

❷ The trick is to follow the original figure-of-eight knot, but backwards.

❸ Make sure the rope follows exactly the same path as the original figure-of-eight and pull the tail through.

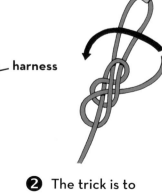

❹ Again, at the finish it should look like a number 8.

PRUSIK HITCH

The prusik is an essential mountaineering knot to master. It is used to attach a loop of cord to a length of rope. Once attached, the loop can be slid up the rope but will not slip when the loop is pulled downwards, which only tightens the knot. Two prusik knots (one for your feet, one clipped into the harness) are often used to climb up, or 'prusik', a rope.

▲ As a climber, you learn the importance of a well-tied knot!

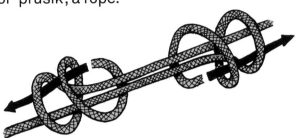

❶ First of all, create a loop of cord by wrapping one end of the cord around the other twice, then passing the end back through the loops, away from the knot's centre. Do this to both ends of the cord.

❷ This should form two X shapes, which will then slide together as you pull the ends of the cord.

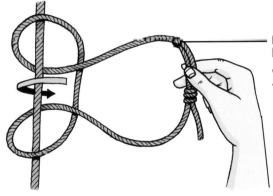

prusik cord must have a smaller diameter than the main rope

❸ Wrap the loop you have just made around the rope you want to climb, and back through itself.

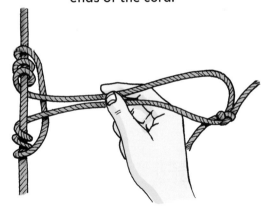

❹ Repeat this process twice more so there is a triple loop at both the top and bottom.

❺ Push the knot together. It will slide up, but will hold if force is applied downwards.

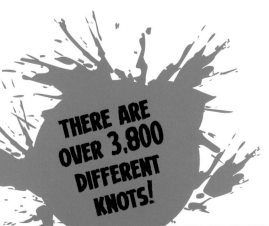

THERE ARE OVER 3,800 DIFFERENT KNOTS!

CLIMBING EVEREST

EVEREST IS AN INCREDIBLE 8,848 M HIGH!

Known as the 'roof of the world', Everest is the highest peak on the planet. Ever since I broke my back in a parachute accident when I was just 22, I had been determined to prove my physical and mental strength by climbing Everest. I finally got my chance in 1998.

BASE CAMP

Base Camp is a tented village over 5,000 m up the slopes of Everest. It is where climbers assemble and spend time getting used to the thin air, which makes it hard to breathe – and for your body to function at all. When my team and I arrived, there were more than 40 climbers in camp: men and women ready, as I was, to risk everything to reach the top. We spent weeks at Base Camp watching the clouds, waiting for the perfect weather window to start our ascent.

▲ We had no idea what the mountain had in store for us.

THE CLIMB

On 7th April, we finally set off to chase our dream. We were climbing with a Sherpa named Nima. The local Sherpa people are the not-so-secret weapon in every attempt to scale Everest. They have adapted to living at high altitude, and are undoubtedly the greatest mountaineers in the world. With oxygen masks on, we climbed higher and higher, through the deadly Khumbu Icefall, over deep crevasses, and up the Lhotse face – a sheer wall of blue ice. Every step was an effort, and all the while we risked avalanches, storms, and deadly falls.

▲ No matter how many times you cross a crevasse by ladder, your heart is always in your mouth!

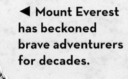

◄ Mount Everest has beckoned brave adventurers for decades.

THE SUMMIT

We made our final make-or-break attempt on the summit on 26th May. It was pitch dark when we left our last camp, at 8,000 m. We climbed up and up, gasping for breath despite our oxygen masks. The final 120 m ridge was like walking on a knife blade. I made the mistake of looking down! Every step was terrifying. But I kept going. Then, finally, at 7.22am, we crested the summit. We had made it!

▼ With freezing winds and so little oxygen that your brain cells are dying with every second, Everest is still one of the most amazing places on Earth.

MOUNTAIN PUZZLES

Find out a little more about animals that live in mountain ranges, from Asia's towering Himalayas to South America's super-long Andes. Grab a pencil and have a go at these games!

DOT TO DOT

Complete the dot to dot to reveal an animal that lives on the lower slopes of mountains.

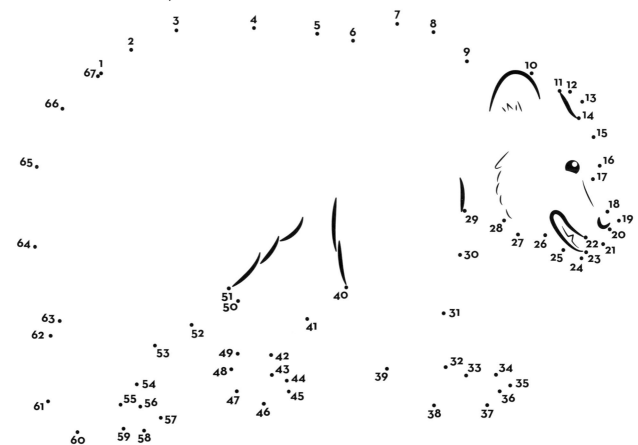

SET UP CAMP

Mountain climbers need to set up camp, and a tent can be a warm and welcoming place after a hard day's trekking. Use the grid to copy this picture of a mountainside campsite. Draw a picture of yourself next to the tent, by the campfire.

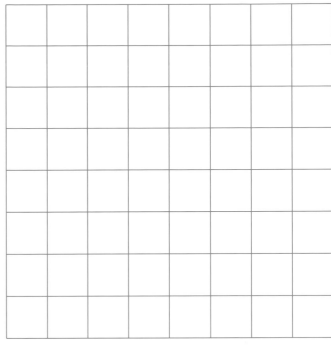

MAKE A WORD

Use the first letter from each animal's name to create a word that means an animal's home.

①
_ARE

②
_LPACA

③
_LACK BEAR

④
_BEX

⑤
_IGER

⑥
_NT

⑦
_AKIN

The hidden word is:

FIRST AID

Unfortunately, it is very common for people to become unwell or get involved in an accident in the mountains. If you are keen to explore, it is important to understand some basic first aid.

CPR

CPR (cardio pulmonary resuscitation) is carried out when somebody falls unconscious and stops breathing. Only ever practise CPR on a dummy – never on your friends, as it would be extremely dangerous. The best place to learn CPR is a specialised first aid course.

❶ Put the heel of your hand on the breastbone at the centre of the patient's chest. Put your other hand on top and lock your fingers together.

❷ Make sure your shoulders are above your arms.

❸ Use your body weight to press straight down on their chest by about 5 cm.

❹ Keep your hands on their chest but relieve the pressure, allowing your hands to come back to their original position.

❺ Repeat this about twice per second until the ambulance arrives.

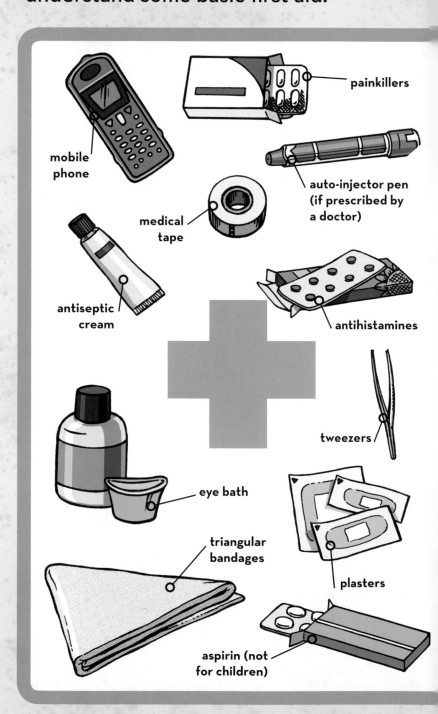

mobile phone

painkillers

auto-injector pen (if prescribed by a doctor)

medical tape

antiseptic cream

antihistamines

tweezers

eye bath

triangular bandages

plasters

aspirin (not for children)

FIRST AID KIT

It is useful to have at least a basic first aid kit for any outdoor situation. You will need to decide what to bring according to the activities you are planning, the time of year, the length of time you are out, and the needs of the people going with you.

THE DEADLIEST MOUNTAIN IS ANNAPURNA IN NEPAL!

disposable gloves

thermometer

scissors

insect repellent

asthma inhaler (if prescribed by a doctor)

eye drops

antiseptic wipes

crêpe rolled bandages

safety pins

sterile eye dressing

small, medium, and large sterile gauze dressings

ACCIDENT RESPONSE

If someone has an accident, remember the following steps:

Danger
Keep yourself safe – you cannot help if you are injured too.

Response
Ask the person their name or tell them to open their eyes to see if they are conscious. It's OK to shout.

Shout for help
Get someone else to call the emergency services (999) while you carry out the first aid.

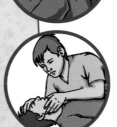

Airway
Make sure their airway isn't blocked and is open. If they are unconscious, tilt their head back and lift their chin.

Breathing
Look, listen, and feel for signs of breathing for 10 seconds. If the casualty is unconscious and not breathing, call for an ambulance and start CPR.

Circulation
Check for a pulse on their wrist or the side of their neck for 10 seconds. Look for signs of bleeding – don't worry about minor cuts. Press down on any bad cuts with a clean pad and raise them above the heart if possible.

Extreme Animals

MOUNTAIN GOATS CAN LEAP 3.6 M IN ONE BOUND!

Only the hardiest animals can deal with the freezing winds and slippery slopes on the world's highest peaks. Mountain animals have developed some extraordinary features and survival strategies, from thick fur to long hibernations through the winter cold.

MOUNTAIN GOAT

These goats can climb the steepest cliffs thanks to their muscular legs and wide hooves, with two toes that spread wide to improve balance. Rough pads on the bottom of each toe provide the grip of a climbing shoe! These goats eat tough mountain plants such as fir trees, and can even find food in the snow.

GRIZZLY BEAR

Known to scientists as the North American brown bear, this giant hibernates for around six months every winter. Grizzlies can be aggressive to humans, particularly when defending their young. However, most of them will avoid humans, and problems usually only occur when they are surprised at very close range.

CONDOR

The two species of condor are the largest flying land birds in the western hemisphere. The California condor can have a wingspan of nearly 3 m. Condors feed on carrion, such as dead goats.

MOUNTAIN QUAIL

These birds are easily recognisable by the distinctive feathers on their heads. They live on the ground in the foothills of mountains. In winter, they migrate short distances down the mountain by foot.

MOUNT GRAHAM RED SQUIRREL

These tiny squirrels live in a remote mountain range in Arizona, USA. They don't hibernate, but they always carry out their main activity during the warmest part of the day, which is midday.

MOUNT LYELL SHREW

At just 10 cm long, this is one of the smallest animals living at high altitude. Because of the amount of energy needed to survive in these conditions, it needs to eat every 1–3 hours and can eat its own body weight in food in one sitting.

If you are walking in the mountains, keep these bear-safety tips in mind:

❶ Keep all food packed away – bears have a very strong sense of smell.

❷ If you spot a bear, stay calm and quiet. Do not react unless you are sure the bear is charging at you.

❸ Talk in a low voice and wave your arms slowly so the bear knows you are human, not prey.

❹ A bright, loud bear banger or attack alarm might scare them off.

❺ If it is dark, shine a torch in their eyes. Their eyesight isn't very good, so this might drive them off.

❻ Find a way to escape the area, but make sure the bear has an escape route too, otherwise it might feel cornered and lash out.

❼ Never walk between a mother bear and her cubs.

❽ If you are charged by a bear, don't run (they can outrun humans) or hide in a tent (they aren't stupid).

❾ If you are attacked, play dead (but never for a polar or black bear). Lie flat on your stomach. Spread your legs out and cover the back of your neck with your hands, locking your fingers together. Use your elbows to cover your face. Stay very still and silent. If the bear does manage to roll you over, roll back onto your stomach again, each time.

bear banger

RAINFORESTS

THE AMAZON RAINFOREST HAS 390 BILLION TREES!

A tropical rainforest is a very tall jungle that gets a lot of rain. The rainforest is very hot and humid, so animals and plants there have learnt to adapt to these conditions. If you want to survive in the rainforest, you will need to put careful planning into staying dry.

◄ I love the wild, weird, and wonderful rainforest, which is filled with more different birds, plants, and animals than anywhere else on Earth.

WHAT IS A RAINFOREST?

Tropical rainforests are found near the Equator, so they have a very hot climate, meaning water evaporates (turns to gas) very quickly. Air can only hold a certain amount of water, so some of the water is pushed back out of the air as rain. In a rainforest, it rains almost every day. The warm, wet climate is perfect for plant growth – and all the plants support a huge number of species of animals!

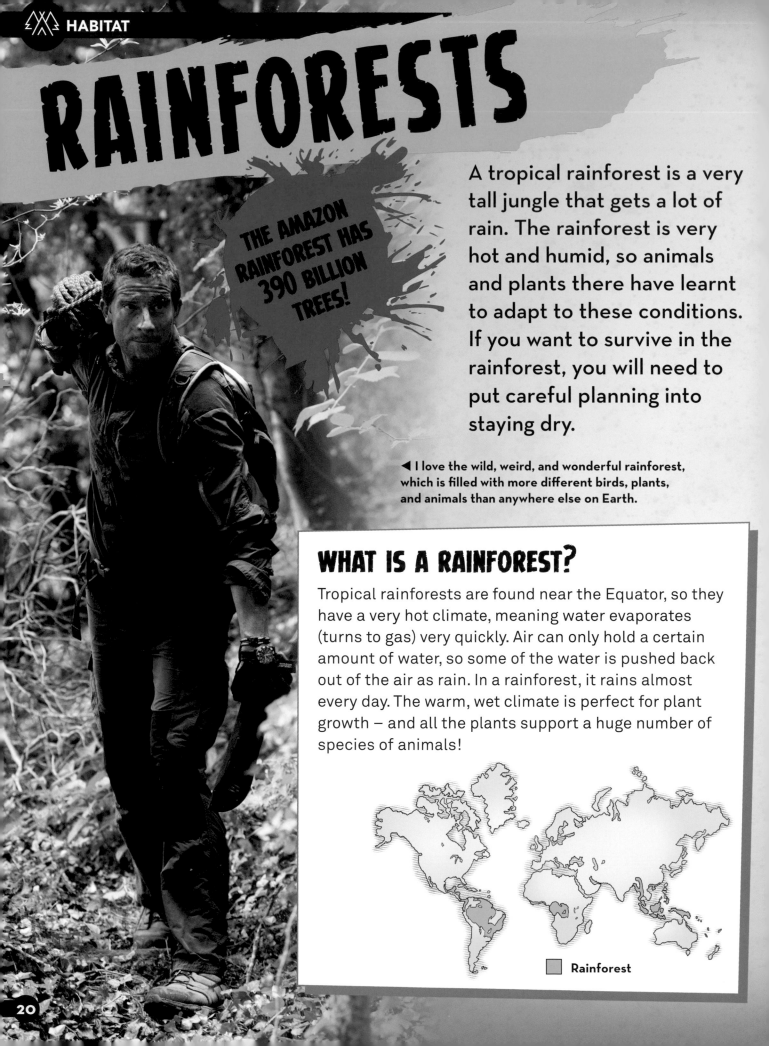

■ Rainforest

macaw

RAINFOREST LAYERS

Tropical rainforests are in four layers. Each layer contains animals and plants that are adapted to the conditions at that level:

The emergent layer

The highest layer is made up of a small number of very large trees that are taller than the rest. Animals that live in the emergent layer often fly or glide about.

sloth

The canopy

This is the roof of the rainforest. Trees in this layer are around 40 m in height. There is plenty of food and sunlight here, so there is a huge diversity of birds and other animals.

spider monkey

The understory

Trees in this layer, such as banana trees, are usually shorter, with large leaves so they can catch as much light as possible.

The forest floor

The bottom layer is deeply shaded by the trees above. Larger animals can move more freely here because there is often not much vegetation.

tarantula

⚠ DANGER: IMMERSION FOOT!

When your feet are continuously in water or mud for more than two days, you can get a condition called immersion foot. It causes blisters and peeling, leaving painful, raw patches that are prone to nasty infections. Often the only way to travel in a rainforest is by foot, so it is essential to keep feet healthy. As soon as you set up camp, spend some time on foot care:

❶ Wash and dry your feet.

❷ Check for blisters or any injuries, and use plasters if necessary.

❸ Use talcum powder to keep feet dry.

❹ Get in a hammock and give your feet plenty of time to rest, and plenty of fresh air.

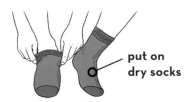
get in a hammock

❺ Spend time drying your wet footwear ready for the next day.

❻ Put on dry socks and/or footwear. Plastic slippers with holes in are useful for around the shelter and are light to carry and fast-drying.

put on dry socks

plastic slippers are useful

SAVING THE RAINFORESTS

Rainforests are in danger! Large areas have been cut down so the trees can be used for timber and the land for farming or construction. Find out more about rainforests at risk with these puzzles.

PROBLEM SOLVER

If a rainforest covered 2.4 million km², and half of it was destroyed by 2050, how much of the rainforest would be left?

$$\frac{2,400,000}{2} = $$

_____ km²

FIND YOUR WORDS

Deforestation is when large areas of forest are destroyed. How many words can you make from the letters in 'DEFORESTATION'?

_____

_____

_____

_____

_____

_____

_____

_____

▼ Around 20 percent of the Amazon has already been lost to deforestation.

IDENTIFY THE ANIMAL

Draw lines to connect each rainforest animal to its name.

QUEEN
ALEXANDRA'S
BIRDWING

SUMATRAN
RHINO

RUFFED
LEMUR

GOLDEN LION
TAMARIN

HELMETED
HORNBILL

SAVE A SPECIES

Use this space to draw and colour a picture of your favourite rainforest animal. Write a sentence explaining why you think its rainforest home should be saved from deforestation.

This animal should be saved from extinction because:

_____

_____

CREEPY CRAWLIES

MOSQUITOES KILL 1 MILLION PEOPLE EVERY YEAR!

It is worth learning about the different creepy crawlies you might come across in the rainforest. Not only are they very interesting, they can also be deadly poisonous, or make a nutritious meal in an emergency situation.

TREMODOTE (FLATWORM)

A tremadote is a small, worm-like creature often found in water. Children who play in dirty water are at risk of getting an infection called snail fever from a particular flatworm. Symptoms include pain, diarrhoea, blood in the faeces and urine, and more serious symptoms if left untreated. Luckily, there is medicine available and, as access to clean water improves, fewer people are getting infected.

MOSQUITO

Mosquitoes consume the blood of other animals. Blood loss isn't usually a problem if you get bitten, as they only drink a few drops, but in some parts of the world mosquitoes can carry nasty diseases such as malaria and zika virus, and may infect you when they bite.

ASSASSIN BUG

The assassin bug is an easily recognisable creature that injects its prey with venom that melts its internal organs. It can kill other, larger bugs, and can give humans a painful bite that may pass on the serious Chagas disease.

AMAZONIAN GIANT CENTIPEDE

This feisty predator will eat anything it can catch – even small snakes and bats. It coils around its prey, eating it alive. It grows to around 30 cm long and will make a human feel unwell if it bites.

BULLET ANT

The bullet ant is one of the most dangerous animals in the rainforest. People who have been bitten say it is as painful as being shot. The place where you are bitten can be paralysed temporarily.

BLOOD-SUCKING LEECHES

If leeches are not removed from the skin, they will fall off when they finish feeding (this takes between 20 minutes and a couple of hours). Leeches produce an anti-clotting agent, so the wound may bleed for some time after the leech has been removed. In addition to stopping the blood from clotting, they also mix it with a chemical to stop it from decaying in their body. This is so efficient that some leeches only need to feed twice a year.

 ## HOW TO SURVIVE LEECHES

If a leech attaches itself to your skin, here is what to do:

❶ Break the leech's seal with your skin using a fingernail or other flat object.

❷ It is not recommended to use chemicals or to burn leeches off, as this causes them to vomit into the wound and may cause an infection.

❸ Clean and dry the wound and apply pressure to stop the bleeding, which may go on for a while.

❹ The wound may itch during healing, so apply a cold pack or ask an adult to give a suitable antihistamine medicine if this is needed.

❺ Some people can have a severe allergic reaction to leech bites, so watch out for any unusual symptoms and ask for medical advice if you are worried.

hold a clean bandage or cloth over a leech wound to stop the bleeding

SHELTERS

In the rainforest it is vital to build a shelter that will protect you from rain! Pick the spot for your camp carefully, away from soft ground, ditches, and gullies, which may turn into a river if it rains.

VERY EARLY HUMANS SLEPT IN TREES FOR SAFETY!

BASIC SHELTER

In an emergency, you can construct this basic lean-to shelter using a poncho. A poncho is a very useful piece of survival equipment. It is a large waterproof sheet with a hole in the middle and an attached hood. You can wear it, wrap things in it, or make it into a shelter. Grommeted corners (with a hole in them) are helpful when attaching it to your structure.

❶ Choose a safe location.

❷ Stretch the poncho out to measure the area of ground to clear.

❸ Move the poncho away and clear the area of debris.

❹ Attach a strong string or rope between two vertical posts or trees about 60 cm off the ground (this will depend on the size of the person).

❺ Attach one of the longer sides of the poncho to the rope – tie with string using the grommets to help.

❻ Attach the other long side of the poncho to the ground. Secure using a tent peg or stake through the grommets, keeping it taut and closing the hood if necessary.

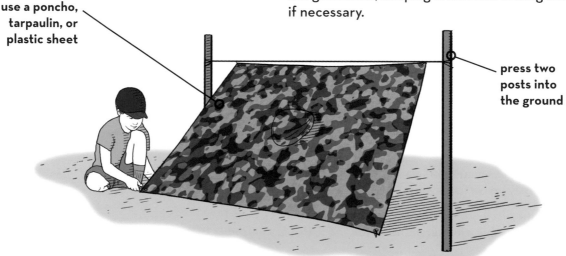

use a poncho, tarpaulin, or plastic sheet

press two posts into the ground

JUNGLE A-FRAME

This more complex shelter will keep you off the forest floor, away from biting insects, scuttling spiders, and snakes.

❶ Take two long, sturdy sticks, connecting them at the top to create an A shape. Secure this with a smaller stick, tied about halfway down. You will need two of these A-shaped frames.

❷ Find three long poles of a similar length. Secure each end of one to the top of your A frames, then rest the other two on the connecting poles to create a hammock area.

❸ Tie the structure securely with rope or string (if you don't have rope, parachute cord or vines will do).

❹ Secure one poncho or tarp as a roof, and the other as a hammock. The hammock will need to be firmly tied, taped, or even sewn, so it can safely hold a person.

rest your A-frames against tree trunks for extra stability

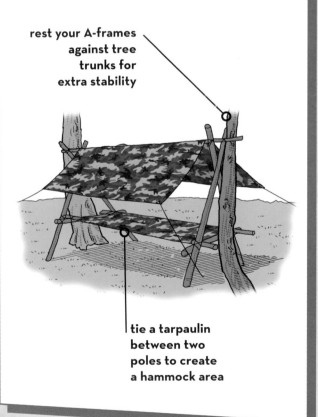

tie a tarpaulin between two poles to create a hammock area

SWAMP BED

Construct this raised bed if the ground is swampy.

❶ Find four trees, or drive posts into the ground to make strong uprights. Make sure there is room for you and your equipment.

❷ Two long poles need to be lashed to the uprights. Make sure they are high enough to keep you dry, allowing for the maximum amount the water will rise.

❸ Tie shorter poles across to form the platform.

❹ Cover the top of the platform with leaves, grass, or any other soft material to make a more comfortable sleeping surface.

soften your bed with moss and leaves

⚠ WATCH FOR TRACKS!

If you would rather not be nibbled during the night, build your shelter away from animal tracks:

❶ Watch out for ant trails and clear away leaves and logs that could shelter spiders or insects.

❷ Look for hoof and paw prints, which could mean your camp is on a route to a waterhole.

LIVINGSTONE IN AFRICA

By the early 19th century, Europeans had explored the coastline of Africa, but the interior of the huge continent was still a mystery to them. Then David Livingstone became the first European to cross Africa from coast to coast.

▲ David Livingstone was one of the most famous explorers in Victorian Britain.

▼ In 1855, Livingstone became the first European to see Victoria Falls on the Zambezi River. Livingstone renamed the falls after the reigning queen of Britain.

BRAVE

In 1841, Livingstone began missionary work in Africa, encouraging people to become Christians. Africa was a dangerous place: there were fierce animals, swamps, dense forests, and deadly diseases such as malaria. Livingstone (sometimes with his wife Mary and their children) was the first European to discover Lake Ngami, cross the Kalahari Desert, and travel across Africa from west to east. When he returned to Britain in 1856, his book about his travels became a bestseller.

THERE ARE MORE THAN 1,250 AFRICAN LANGUAGES!

RESPECTFUL

Livingstone always showed great respect to African people. He studied African languages and cultures, and employed many Africans as guides. He carried few weapons and was careful not to overreact to aggression. Livingstone also saw the results of the slave trade: captives being marched in chains and villages emptied of people. Back at home, he campaigned against the terrible trade.

LIVINGSTONE'S ENCOUNTER WITH A LION.

▲ When Livingstone was attacked by a lion, he was saved by his African friend Mebalwe.

LOST!

In 1866, Livingstone returned to Africa to find the source of the River Nile. Soon his African porters deserted, his supplies were stolen, and he fell ill. After 1867, no news of Livingstone reached the outside world. Search parties went to find him, but returned without success. Finally, in 1871, explorer Henry Morton Stanley found a very tired Livingstone on the shores of Lake Tanganyika.

▲ As Stanley walked up to Livingstone, he raised his hat and said the now-famous words: 'Dr. Livingstone, I presume?'

EDIBLE PLANTS

Plants are the easiest food to gather from the wild. Rainforests offer plenty of plants that are edible, but there are lots of poisonous ones, too. Always take great care when foraging!

PLANT SAFETY

If you are interested in foraging, the best way to learn is to go on an organised course with an expert. Always follow these safety rules:

1 Always check with an adult who knows about plants before touching anything.

ask an adult

2 If you are out exploring with your dog, keep it away from plants.

3 Never eat any plant unless you have been told it is safe by an adult who is experienced in foraging and plant identification.

4 Watch out for thorns, prickles, and the sharp edges of leaves. It is often tempting to run your hands up a tall reed or grass leaf only to get an injury similar to a paper cut.

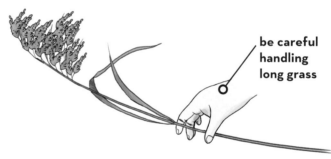

be careful handling long grass

5 Be careful around water – sometimes pond weed can look like grass!

6 Don't rub your eyes – some pollen can be extremely irritating.

7 Wash your hands after touching plants and before eating.

always wash your hands after touching plants

TROPICAL TREATS

sago palm

bamboo shoot

Stems and shoots

Sago palm has a spiny trunk with arching fronds. The spongy inner part can be cooked and eaten. The growing tips of most palms are edible, too. Young bamboo shoots can also be cooked and eaten.

mangoes

soursop

bananas

coconuts

Fruits

Many fruits grow wild in the tropics. Mangoes are large, juicy, peach-coloured fruits. Soursop are green, spiky fruits shaped a little like avocadoes. You many also find bananas, plantains, and coconuts, which are all delicious and safe to eat.

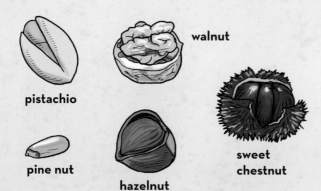

walnut

pistachio

pine nut

hazelnut

sweet chestnut

Nuts

These are packed with healthy fats and protein. Pistachios, walnuts, hazelnuts, and pine nuts are very tasty when cooked, but can also be eaten raw. Sweet chestnuts must be roasted.

▲ Getting enough food is vital on an expedition, as it is the fuel that provides the energy we need to survive.

⚠️ POISONOUS PLANTS

Some plants and many fungi are poisonous. Eating them will make you ill and could be fatal. Here are just some of the many plants that might be deadly:

❶ Many types of fungi (mushrooms and toadstools) are poisonous, so – unless you are with an adult fungi expert – don't ever pick fungi.

❷ Avoid plants with milky sap.

❸ Don't touch plants with tiny barbs on the stems and leaves.

❹ Many red plants are poisonous.

❺ Pick ripe, colourful fruit, not hard, green berries. 90 percent of black or purple berries are edible, but only 50 percent of red berries are.

Deadly fungi

destroying angel

fly agaric

death cap

POLAR LANDS

The poles are the coldest places on Earth and are covered with thick ice all year round. Polar environments are the most challenging places for people to survive. Although we have known that they exist for a long time, they have been explored only within the last 150 years because of the super-tough terrain.

◄ Very few people have ever explored the fascinating polar worlds, but there is so much to discover – you just need to know how!

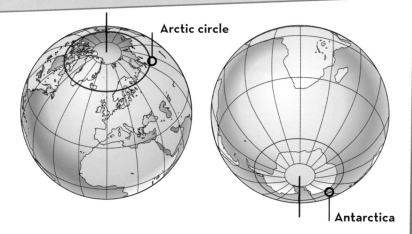

Arctic circle

Antarctica

THE ARCTIC AND ANTARCTICA

The North Pole is covered by thick sea ice floating on the Arctic Ocean. This area is within the Arctic Circle, which is the part of the world that is furthest north. The South Pole is on a continent called Antarctica, which is covered by an ice sheet that contains 70 percent of the Earth's fresh water. Antarctica is Earth's southernmost continent. Though it is freezing cold, it is actually considered the biggest desert in the world due to low rainfall.

Snow cave

Pile up snow to make a mound, packing the snow firmly. If possible, leave the snow for a couple of hours so it can harden. Dig a tunnel into the mound, then hollow out the cave. Smooth the inside to prevent drips. Carve benches and make ventilation holes. Keep your shovels inside with you in case of avalanche.

POLAR SHELTERS

Having the right shelter can save your life. It is important to be out of the wind, as warm as possible, and safe from animal attack. Remember that trapped air can be a good insulator. Building materials may be limited, so you need to be smart:

Snow trench

Dig down about 1 m into the snow, creating a trench long and wide enough to lie down in. Use tarpaulin or evergreen branches to make a roof, making sure there is space for air to get in. Use piles of snow to weigh down your roof material.

Tree pit

Dig down in the snow around the trunk of an evergreen tree. Pack the snow tightly along the sides to make sure they're firm to avoid your shelter caving in. Use branches to sit on and to cover the top of the hole.

⚠ DANGER: THIN ICE!

Falling through thin ice into freezing water can be a very scary experience, but it is important to stay as calm as possible while you try to get to safety:

❶ Keep calm, control your breathing, and make a plan.

❷ Drop any heavy items such as clothing or backpacks – these can be replaced, but you cannot.

❸ If you are alone, shout for help.

❹ Get out of the water as fast as possible because, in cold water, every minute is vital.

❺ If you are underwater, try to get back to where you fell in and climb out. Look for colours – dark ice has snow on top of it and will be harder to break through than light ice.

❻ If you can't get out of the water, try to stay as still as possible, keeping your head, arms, and as much of your body as you can out of the water. Cross your legs if you can.

❼ If you can get out, roll well away from the hole before you attempt to stand up.

❽ Once you are out, remove wet clothing, stay somewhere sheltered, and light a fire. Get help immediately.

Igloo

An igloo will provide excellent shelter, but takes lots of time and energy to build. Pack snow tightly together to create 'bricks'. Stack the bricks in a dome shape, leaving an entranceway, then smooth down the inside walls to prevent drips.

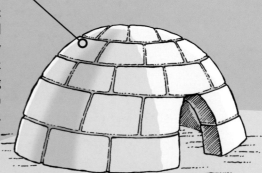

RACE TO THE SOUTH POLE

▼ Amundsen's speedy, cold-adapted sled dogs were a key part of his success. Sadly, some were killed on the way to feed the other dogs.

Antarctica was the last continent to be discovered, and the last to be explored. It wasn't until the end of the nineteenth century that people began to venture onto the frozen, windswept land. In 1911, two very different teams of explorers raced to be the first to reach the South Pole.

IT GETS AS COLD AS -89°C IN ANTARCTICA!

ROALD AMUNDSEN

The Norwegian explorer Amundsen, his men, and their 97 sled-pulling husky dogs reached Antarctica on 11th January 1911. Since the men and their dogs could not drag along all the supplies needed for their journey, they immediately set up a series of buried supply caches part of the way along their planned route to the Pole, marking them with flags. After careful planning, the team set off for the Pole on 19th October. Moving at up to 32 km a day on their skis, the team battled through blizzards – reaching the South Pole on 19th December!

ROBERT FALCON SCOTT

The British explorer Scott, his men, their dogs, ponies and two motor sleds arrived in Antarctica on 4th January 1911. They set off for the Pole on 1st November, moving more slowly than Amundsen's team because the men were not experienced skiiers. The sleds soon broke down, the ponies were shot for food, and the dogs were sent back to base camp. As they made their final push for the Pole, Scott's men moved slowly, dragging their supplies behind them.

◀ Scott's skis and cold-weather clothes were old-fashioned and heavy.

TRAGEDY

Scott and four companions finally reached the Pole on 17th January 1912 – five weeks after Amundsen. On their return journey, they realised their backup team was not going to turn up with extra supplies as they had agreed. They were frostbitten and hungry. Lawrence Oates, one member of Scott's team, became very sick and realised he was slowing his team down. One day, he announced, 'I'm just going outside, and I may be some time,' before walking out into a blizzard, never to be seen again. Eventually, the rest of the men, including Scott, also died. We know all this from the notes they left behind.

▲ Scott and his men took this photograph of themselves at the South Pole. They had seen the Norwegian flag planted by Amundsen, so they knew they were beaten.

▼ Almost all (98 percent) of Antarctica is covered by ice, much of it more than 2.5 km thick.

STAYING WARM

When adventuring in icy conditions, you need to wear the right clothes to stay warm. All of your extremities – hands, feet, and even your nose – will need to be covered to prevent frostbite. Yet sometimes even the warmest clothing is not enough, so take note of these essential survival tips!

NORMAL BODY TEMPERATURE IS 37°C !

COLD DANGERS

Every cold-weather adventurer needs to be able to spot the symptoms of these dangerous conditions:

slurred speech
shallow breathing
weak pulse
shivering
confusion
clumsiness

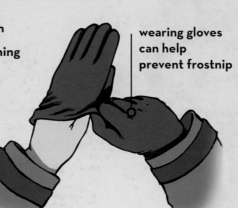

wearing gloves can help prevent frostnip

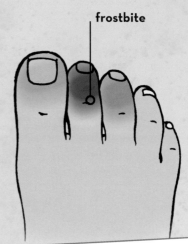

frostbite

Hypothermia

This very dangerous condition occurs when your body temperature drops below 35°C. Symptoms vary, but can include shivering, shallow breathing, slurred speech and, in extreme cases, loss of consciousness and even death. If you suspect someone has hypothermia, get them immediate medical attention.

Frostnip

This is an early stage of frostbite, so it is important to recognise the signs and do something before the situation becomes serious. Symptoms include pins and needles, throbbing, and aching. It is most likely to affect fingers, nose, ears, and toes. The affected area may become numb and white but there should be no lasting damage if you catch it early.

Frostbite

This is a very serious condition and urgent medical attention is required, as muscle and bones can be permanently damaged. The skin becomes blotchy and turns white or blue. As the skin thaws, blisters filled with blood may develop and some tissue may die and have to be removed. Explorers have lost fingers, toes, and other body parts to frostbite.

SURVIVAL TIPS

Wear the right clothing

Preparation is key for survival in cold weather. The correct equipment and clothing are vital. Base layer clothing traps air as insulation, while a waterproof outer layer stops you losing heat. Stay covered at all times – even the tip of your nose needs to stay out of the elements. You lose a lot of heat from your head, so pay particular attention to keeping it warm.

waterproof trousers

jacket

down mittens

balaclava

Fuel up on food

Fatty food and plenty of warm drinks will keep the body fuelled. Some people eat up to eight bars of chocolate a day, because staying warm uses up lots of energy. You also need to drink plenty of water – the air in Antarctica is so dry that you will lose water just from breathing.

Beware the wind!

Heat can be transferred in a liquid or a gas, such as water or air. This process is called 'convection'. Moving air will pull heat away from your body faster than still air, which is why it is harder to stay warm if it is windy. Keeping your whole body covered will help prevent heat loss through convection. If you need to rest, choose a sheltered spot.

Do not touch the snow

When two solid materials are touching each other, heat will travel from the hotter material to the cooler one until both objects are the same temperature. This process is called 'conduction'. Try not to touch anything cold directly, in order to keep heat in your body. So do not sit down on the snow. And do not play snowballs!

WINTER WARMERS

If you go on a polar expedition, you will need to be just as hardy as polar animals. In addition, you will need to be armed with keen navigation and problem-solving skills.

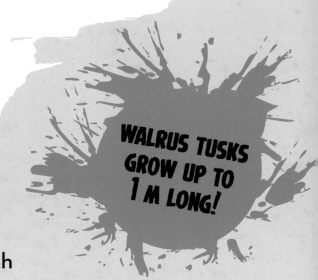

WALRUS TUSKS GROW UP TO 1 M LONG!

FIND NORTH

If you ever get lost at night, you can use the stars to help you find north. The North Star is above the North Pole and stays in one spot, so you can use it to figure out which way is north – just look for the star constellations known as the Little and Big Dippers. Join the dots to reveal the Dippers and colour in the North Star so you will always remember where it is!

1 • North Star

5 •
6 •

2 •
3 •   **Little Dipper**   **Big Dipper**   7 •

4 •   8 •

4 •

3 •

5 •
9 •   6 •   2 •

8 •

7 •   1 •

SCRAMBLED ANIMALS

Unscramble the names of these animals that live in polar places.

❶ EASL

_____

❷ ENUPGIN

_____

❸ SUKM XOEN

_____

❹ APLRO EABR

_____

❺ CRAO

_____

❻ LRWUAS

_____

SURVIVAL STRATEGIES

Many Arctic animals have a thick layer of fat, called blubber, or long shaggy fur that helps keep them warm. Name the animals (there are hints in another puzzle on this page!), read the clues, and draw a line to the correct animal.

I have white fur and massive claws that help me catch seals.

I have a bushy tail that I wrap around my body for warmth.

I am very fat and have long whiskers and two long tusks.

I have layers of thick shaggy fur and horns on my head.

I spend a lot of time underwater hiding from polar bears.

❶

❷

❸

❹

❺

POLAR NIGHT AND DAY

Polar animals have to deal with extreme winters and summers. At the North Pole, the sun rarely sets in the summer. In the winter, the sun almost never rises. If there are 18 hours of sunlight in a day, how many hours of darkness will there be? What season would it be?

The season would be _____ .

There are _____ hours of darkness.

POLAR LIFE

There are very few animals that live in the Antarctic all year round, because the winter conditions are so harsh. Most animals live near the coast, hunting in the icy waters. The Arctic has far more animals, as it can be reached from surrounding areas by land.

EMPEROR PENGUINS CAN REACH 122 CM IN HEIGHT!

SOUTHERN ELEPHANT SEAL

The southern elephant seal is the biggest seal in the world – males can grow to 6 m. It comes ashore to rest in Antarctica. It mainly eats squid, which makes its breath smell disgusting!

chinstrap penguin in a stone nest

male emperor penguins looking after their eggs

king penguin and chick

PENGUINS

All these flightless birds live in the Southern Hemisphere, except the Galapagos penguin, which is found just north of the Equator. Penguins spend half their lives on land and the other half in water, hunting for fish. Species that live in or near Antarctica include emperor, chinstrap, and king penguins.

ARCTIC HARE

Arctic hares have thick fur to help them keep warm, and around 20 percent of their body mass is fat, which is a good insulator. They have heavily padded paws to stop them sliding around on the ice or sinking in the snow.

WOLVERINE

They might look cuddly, but these members of the weasel family can tackle animals far larger than themselves. Wolverines live in the Arctic, as well as forests just further south.

ARCTIC FOX

These foxes have white fur to camouflage them in the snow, but they are sometimes hunted for their beautiful coats. They hunt small animals, especially lemmings. The Arctic fox is Iceland's only native mammal.

SURVIVE A POLAR BEAR ATTACK

Polar bears are found all around the Arctic coast. Clever hunters with an amazing sense of smell, they are extremely dangerous and have been known to attack humans. Avoid them as much as possible and follow these survival tips:

1 Set up electric fences around your camp.

2 A dog will alert you if a bear is nearby, and the barking may scare the bear away.

3 If you see a bear, make yourself look as big as possible, and make a lot of noise. Try banging on metal pots.

4 Guns can be effective, but not always. To kill a bear, the bullet needs to hit its brain.

BELUGA WHALE

Belugas use echolocation to find their way under the Arctic ice. They make a noise, and can tell what is nearby by the way the sound echoes back off objects.

CAMPFIRE COOKING

HUMANS FIRST LIT FIRES 600,000 YEARS AGO!

Fire-making and campfire cooking are great fun, but can also be dangerous. Take a lot of care around fires, and never leave a fire unattended. Always have a bucket of water or fire blanket handy.

GATHER MATERIALS

Assemble all the materials you need: tinder will take the spark and kindling will feed the flames. You will then need wood of different thicknesses to fuel the fire.

❶ Tinder: Dry grass, straw, birch bark, sawdust, pine needles, animal fur, tissue paper, and scrunched-up newspaper all make good tinder when bone dry.

❷ Kindling: Dry twigs about 2 cm across make good kindling. You can also use wood shavings, or split dry softwood with an axe.

❸ Fuel: Feed the fire with small logs or split wood, then larger logs.

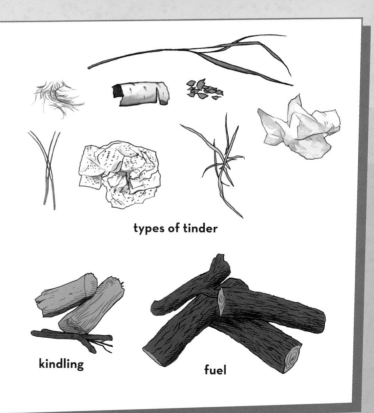

types of tinder

kindling

fuel

CHOOSE YOUR LOCATION

Build your fire on level ground, away from trees or overhanging branches. Site it well away from tents and downwind of your campsite, otherwise you risk drifting sparks igniting the fabric. Clear the ground of sticks and moss that could cause the fire to spread.

LIGHT YOUR FIRE

use a match or lighter to light the tinder

❶ Build a small tepee of sticks with a ball of tinder in the centre. Leave gaps so that air can reach the tinder.

❷ Strike a match or put a lighter to the tinder. If you are using matches, always strike in the direction away from your body. Cup your hands around the flame to shield it from wind.

❸ Blow gently to fan the ember. After the tinder has caught fire, add small and then larger sticks to feed the flames.

add larger sticks to feed the flames

COOKING METHODS

adjust the heat by raising or lowering your pot

remember to turn the spit

Spit roast

Meat, fish, and other foods can be roasted on a spit. Use green wood to make the spit, as it is less likely to catch fire. Turn the spit regularly to make sure food is cooked evenly.

Tripod

You will need three long, straight sticks. Bind one end of the sticks together with cord, and fan out the other ends and adjust to form a stable, three-legged structure. Hang a hook from the cord, then hang a pot or kettle from the hook.

⚠ PUT IT OUT!

Allow the fire to burn right down, then sprinkle water over the embers or smother them with earth to make sure the fire is fully out.

cook foil packages in the embers

keep a bucket of water, sand, or earth nearby

Baked in foil

Fish, meat, potatoes, and fruit all taste great baked in foil in the embers of a campfire. Thick foil is best as it won't tear. Wrap the foil around your food to form an airtight package. Use tongs to place it in and remove it from the fire, then open the package with care.

DESERTS

THE DRIEST DESERT IS THE ATACAMA IN SOUTH AMERICA!

Almost one third of the world's surface is desert. Deserts have less than 25 cm of rainfall per year, and these unforgiving landscapes can be either baking hot or mind-numbingly freezing! In order to survive here, you need to have some special know-how and well-practised survival skills.

▼ The desert can be an unforgiving place, so it is vital you are properly prepared before any adventure.

WHAT IS A DESERT?

Most people think of deserts as hot places, but temperatures vary widely, with extreme cold and high winds at night. A hot desert is Africa's Sahara, while a cold desert is Asia's Gobi. Why do deserts get so little rain? Some deserts are ringed by mountains. These mountains force the rain-bringing winds to cool, which forms clouds. This means the rain falls before the moisture reaches the desert. Other deserts are near the Equator, in a region where the air is very dry.

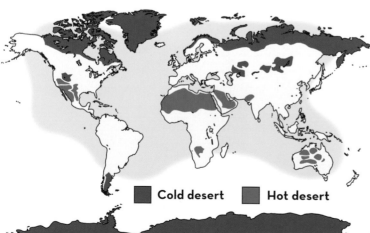

■ Cold desert   ■ Hot desert

DESERT PLANTS

It is often thought that plants cannot grow in a desert environment – this isn't true. There are actually many different plants that are adapted to survive with small amounts of water.

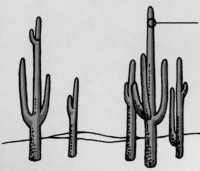

Saguaro cactus

This cactus can grow over 20 m tall and live for over 150 years. Native to Arizona, US, it survives hot weather and droughts by storing water – it visibly expands after rain. The fruits are edible, but you would need a very long pole to get them.

Living stone

These plants get their name from their stone-like appearance. They can survive blazing-hot deserts by partially burying themselves underground. In times of drought, the plant can bury itself further until it is completely covered, allowing it to survive even the most extreme conditions.

Desert marigold

This plant has very hairy leaves that are essential for its survival. The leaves increase the amount of light reflected, which then lowers the leaf temperature and blocks harmful UV light. These flowers are extremely poisonous!

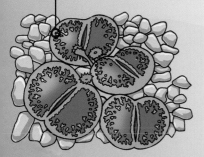

Ghost flower

Unlike most plants, the ghost flower does not get its energy from sunlight, but feeds off fungi. It is sometimes completely white and can also grow in very dark environments. It often flowers a few days after rainfall and only has one flower per stem.

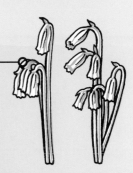

⚠ DANGER: SANDSTORM!

Sandstorms happen when the wind picks up sand. They can be very scary, as you cannot see anything and your eyes, mouth, and nose are coated in sand. Try these survival tips:

❶ Listen to local TV or radio information for sandstorm warnings.

❷ Always carry a blanket, goggles, mask, and water in the desert.

❸ Put a mask or damp cloth over your nose and mouth.

❹ Wear goggles, or shield your eyes with your arm, and then wrap a cloth around your eyes and ears.

❺ Find shelter as quickly as possible. If there is no shelter nearby, crouch down low.

❻ Keep as much skin and face covered as possible.

❼ If you are with a camel, get it to sit down and press yourself against its sheltered side – camels are good at coping with sandstorms.

❽ Stay where you are until the storm passes.

shelter behind your camel

DESERT LIFE

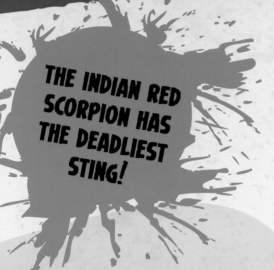

THE INDIAN RED SCORPION HAS THE DEADLIEST STING!

Deserts have extreme temperatures and little to no water. Animals that have made their homes in deserts have evolved features, such as humps and large tails, that help to keep them cool and and hydrated. They have also developed some amazing survival tools and instincts!

AFRICAN PYXIE FROG

It used to be thought that these frogs died off in the dry season, but scientists have discovered that they actually bury themselves and create a cocoon that hardens around their body. They can hibernate in this cocoon for up to seven years. When it finally rains, the moisture makes the cocoon soften and the frog wakes up.

THORNY DEVIL

This lizard has special skin that can gather all the water it needs directly from rain, standing water, and soil moisture. Its skin has a special ability to absorb water it comes into contact with, and it has scales that channel water to the corners of its mouth.

CAMEL

Most of the camels in the world are dromedary camels with one hump. Only six percent of camels have two humps. Many people believe that camels store water in their hump. This is a common myth – the hump actually stores the camel's fat. By storing fat in the hump instead of around their body, camels are able to stay cool in the heat. Camels don't even need to drink water if there is none available, instead getting their water from green plants.

ORYX

These large antelopes feed in the early morning and late afternoon when desert temperatures are low. Oryx have an amazing ability – they can regulate their body temperature to stop sweating. By doing this they can preserve a lot of valuable water.

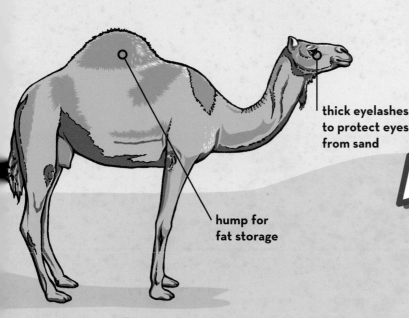

thick eyelashes to protect eyes from sand

hump for fat storage

⚠ SCORPION STINGS!

Desert scorpions are nocturnal and often hide under rocks during the day, so take care when moving rocks. If someone is stung by a scorpion, always call for medical assistance, describing the scorpion if at all possible. Then take these steps:

❶ Keep the victim calm.

❷ Wash and dry the stung area.

❸ Use ice to keep the swelling down.

❹ Keep the stung area below heart level to slow down the spread of venom.

❺ Ask an adult for a suitable painkiller.

❻ Watch out for the signs of an allergic reaction. If the person stops breathing, follow first aid procedures, performing CPR and rescue breaths if necessary.

SIDEWINDER RATTLESNAKE

These snakes are named after the track they leave in the sand when they move. They are also known as horned rattlesnakes as they have little bumps that look like horns above their eyes. They give a venomous bite which should be treated urgently.

SOS!

SEMAPHORE WAS INVENTED IN FRANCE IN 1792!

SOS is an internationally recognised distress call. The letters stand for 'Save Our Souls'. Distress signals are used to call for help in an emergency. Rescuers will risk their own lives to answer distress calls. These signals are taken very seriously, so should never be misused.

MAKE LETTERS

If someone is injured, ill, or lost, you may need to signal for help. Try spelling out the letters 'SOS' using one of these methods:

Spelling it out

To draw attention to your location from the air, natural materials such as rocks, pebbles, and branches can be used to spell out SOS or HELP. You can also draw letters in snow, mud, and sand. Letters should be at least 10 m tall, 3 m wide, and 3 m apart to be seen from the air.

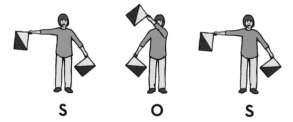

S   O   S

Semaphore

Semaphore is a system of signalling using flags to spell letters and words. Semaphore was widely used by sailors in past centuries and is still used today. You can improvise flags using brightly coloured cloths or clothing.

three short   three long   three short

Morse code

Morse code is an international code made up of short signals, or 'dots', and longer signals, or 'dashes'. Developed in the 1830s, it is named after American inventor Samuel Morse. Different combinations of dots and dashes represent numbers and letters of the alphabet. Morse code messages can be sent using visual signals such as smoke, flags, and light flashes, or you can use audio signals such as whistle blasts or beeps on a radio.

ANY WAY YOU CAN

Signal to aircraft

In an emergency you can signal an aircraft using a mirror. This method only works when it's sunny.

❶ Hold the mirror at shoulder height and point it towards the sun.

❷ Stretch your other arm out with two fingers up and palm facing inwards. Sight the aircraft (or another target) between your fingers.

❸ Angle the mirror so a spot of reflected light hits your fingers.

❹ Lower your outstretched hand while keeping the mirror at the same angle to direct the flash at the plane.

▲ If you are lost, injured, or the weather takes a turn for the worse, knowing how to use the resources around you to signal for help could be a life-saving skill.

Make a flag

You can improvise a flag from brightly coloured clothing, a space blanket, sleeping bag, or life jacket tied to a stick. Wave the flag above your head if help is in sight.

Three for danger

Any signal repeated three times is an internationally recognised distress call. This includes three blasts of a whistle, three light flashes, or three fires, arranged in a line or triangle.

CROSSING AUSTRALIA

ABORIGINES HAVE LIVED IN AUSTRALIA FOR 70,000 YEARS!

After the first European settlers arrived in Australia in 1788, explorers began to travel inland, but 70 years later no one had yet crossed the vast, dry interior. On 20th August 1860, an expedition led by Robert O'Hara Burke set out from Melbourne in southern Australia, heading north.

▼ The expedition's leader, Robert O'Hara Burke, was a poor leader with no experience of exploration.

▼ The Australian desert, known as the Outback, is a beautiful but harsh land, with very little food and water.

SETTING OFF

Burke set out from Melbourne with 18 men, 23 horses, and 25 camels. The camels, just imported from India, were among the first seen in Australia. The plan was to travel north along the Darling River at first, then hit the north coast at the Gulf of Carpentaria. When the expedition got to the halfway point, at Cooper's Creek, William Brahe and most of the men were ordered to set up camp and wait with supplies.

DELAY, DELAY, DELAY

Burke, William Wills, Charles Gray, and John King headed north from Cooper Creek. Quarrels, bad luck, and rains led to delay after delay. They finally reached the mouth of the Flinders River, at the Gulf of Carpentaria, on 9th February 1861, but did not see the ocean as they were cut off by swamp. The men knew they had enough supplies for five weeks but the trip back to Cooper's Creek would take 10 weeks. They set off immediately. Gray soon died from exhaustion. Burke, Wills, and King were very weak when they reached Cooper's Creek on 21st April. Unfortunately, Brahe's team – who were running low on their own supplies – had left the day before.

▲ Staying alive in the Outback requires the right equipment and knowledge - which the explorers did not have, unlike the continent's Aboriginal peoples.

THE WORST LUCK

Burke, Wills, and King headed for home only hours behind Brahe. At first they were helped by Aboriginal Australians, who gave them food and water. When this ran out, they ate their last two camels. A month later, the exhausted men found themselves back at Cooper's Creek —they had walked in circles. Again, they had just missed Brahe, who had returned to look for them. Confused and despairing, the three men set out again. Burke and Wills died in June or July. With the help of Aborigines, King survived until 18th September, when he was found by a rescue party.

▲ Burke, Wills, and King were devastated when they returned to Cooper's Creek to find the camp deserted.

HEATING UP

Have a go at these perplexing puzzles to find out more about some of the resourceful animals and people that live in deserts!

MEERKAT MADNESS

Can you spot five differences between these two pictures of meerkats?

SECRET ANIMAL

Use the secret code to discover the name of a burrowing desert animal.

A	B	C	D	E	F	G	H	I	J	K	L	M	N	O	P	Q	R	S	T	U	V	W	X	Y	Z
1	2	3	4	5	6	7	8	9	10	11	12	13	14	15	16	17	18	19	20	21	22	23	24	25	26

7 18 15 21 14 4   19 17 21 9 18 18 5 12

__ __ __ __ __ __   __ __ __ __ __ __ __ __

Can you write your name using the secret code?

CAMEL DISCOVERER

Here are some key facts about Bactrian camels and dromedaries.
Use the fact box to answer the questions below.

	Bactrian camels	Dromedaries
Weight	Up to 700 kg	Up to 550 kg
Length	Up to 300 cm	Up to 340 cm
Location	Asia	Asia and Africa
How many humps?	2	1

1 Where would you find Bactrian camels – Asia, Africa, or both?

2 Which type of camel is heaviest, a Bactrian or a dromedary?

3 If you had five Bactrian camels and six dromedaries, how many humps would there be altogether?

4 Which type of camel is the longest?

ABORIGINAL ART

The Aboriginal people are the native peoples of Australia. They know the land well and are experts at surviving in the Outback. They have a unique and beautiful form of art called dot painting, where they use hundreds of tiny dots to create a picture. Fill in the image below using the colour guide on the right to make your own dot painting.

FINDING WATER

Water is more important than food in a survival situation. In the desert, where water is scarce, staying hydrated is a major safety concern. Humans can live for weeks without food, but without water you can die in a few days – even in fairly cool conditions.

DEHYDRATION

Why is water important?

Water keeps us the correct temperature, moves substances around our bodies, and helps to get rid of waste. We cannot live for more than about 3–5 days without water.

What is dehydration?

Dehydration is when someone loses more fluid through sweating, vomiting, diarrhoea, or urinating than they have taken in from eating and drinking.

How can it be treated?

You should treat dehydration by drinking plenty of water, taking a rehydration solution (you can buy this in sachets from a chemist), resting, and massaging cramped muscles. If the person doesn't get better fast – get them to a doctor.

◄ The signs of dehydration include headache, dry mouth, small amounts of dark urine, and muscle cramps.

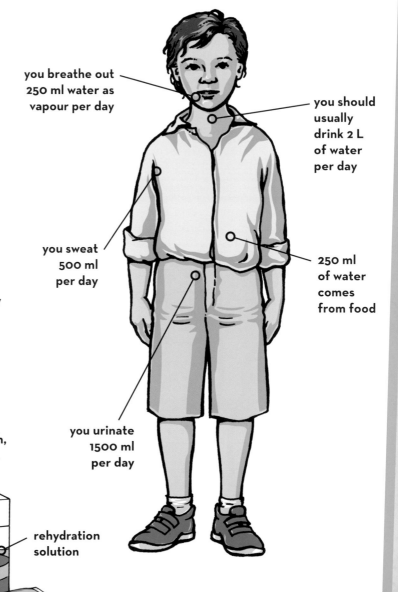

you breathe out 250 ml water as vapour per day

you should usually drink 2 L of water per day

you sweat 500 ml per day

250 ml of water comes from food

you urinate 1500 ml per day

rehydration solution

DESERT WATER

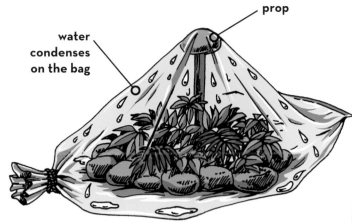

water condenses on the bag

prop

Find an oasis

An oasis is an isolated place in a desert where there is water, and plants grow. Animals and humans often make habitats at an oasis if it is large enough to support the group. The water is from an underground river reaching the surface and forming a spring, pond, or lake.

Collect water from cuttings

Place as many plant cuttings as possible in a bag – just make sure they don't touch the sides. Prop up the centre of the bag to form a tent shape. Put the bag on a slope so that the water can run to a corner to make collection easy.

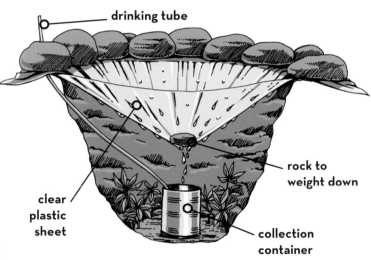

drinking tube

clear plastic sheet

rock to weight down

collection container

Watch for wings

If you see bees, flies, mosquitoes, or frogs you are likely to be less than 5 km from water.

Make a solar still

Dig a hole and place some plants in it. Put a clean cup or bowl in the hole to collect water. Spread a plastic sheet over the hole, weighted down by rocks, with one small rock in the centre to create a dip. Moisture will slowly evaporate from the plants, rise, and condense on the underside of the plastic sheet. It will drip into the collection container. Water can be drunk without disturbing the system by using a drinking tube.

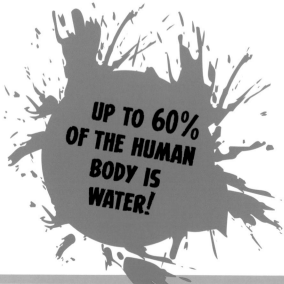

UP TO 60% OF THE HUMAN BODY IS WATER!

BY THE SEA

The oceans cover about 70 percent of Earth and, at their deepest, go down almost 11 km. That's a big place to explore! The watery world under the surface of the ocean is still one of the most mysterious parts of our planet – even after lots of exploring, we haven't found out everything there is to know.

▼ Our coasts are the most mind-blowing places to explore, but watch out for powerful tides and unpredicatable weather!

THE PACIFIC OCEAN HAS 135,000 KM OF COASTLINE!

THE FIVE OCEANS

Geographers divide the planet's salty water into five oceans. From the largest to smallest they are the Pacific, Atlantic, Indian, Antarctic (sometimes called the Southern), and Arctic Oceans. A sea is the name for an area of salty water that is partly or fully enclosed by land, such as the Mediterranean Sea, which is bordered by southern Europe, western Asia, and northern Africa.

Arctic

Atlantic

Pacific

Indian

Pacific

Antarctic

OCEAN LIFE

Seawater is a huge potion of water, salt, tiny grains of rock, and billions of animals and plants. All these creatures are adapted to survive in particular conditions, from the warm, shallow waters of a coral reef to the dark, deep oceans.

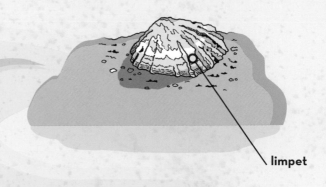

limpet

seagull

Coasts

A coast is where the land meets the sea, creating amazing landscapes, from cliffs and sandy beaches to salty swamps and seagrass beds. Battered by waves and winds, coasts are always changing. The animals and plants that live here have to cope with extreme conditions.

The open ocean

The smallest fish is tinier than a fingernail, and the biggest is the whale shark, which can grow to more than 10 m long. Yet there is plenty more than fish in the sea, including mammals, such as whales, and invertebrates, such as jellyfish. Light cannot pass through the water beyond a depth of about 1,000 m. Some deep-sea creatures make their own light, a skill called bioluminescence.

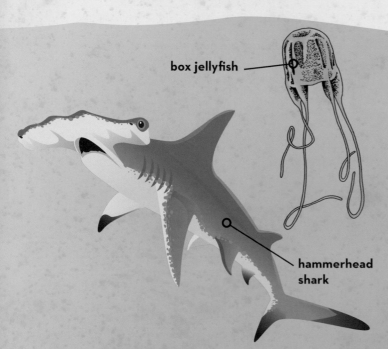

box jellyfish

hammerhead shark

⚠ DANGER: SWIMMING!

Swimming in the sea is more fun than just about anything else, but it can be very dangerous! Take note of these essential survival tips:

❶ Only ever swim at a lifeguarded beach and stick within the flags set out by lifeguards to mark which area is safe.

❷ Never swim alone.

❸ Be aware of your swimming ability, as open water is more dangerous than a swimming pool. So stay very close to shore.

❹ Be aware of rip currents, which are narrow, powerful bands of water that flow quickly away from the shore and can drag you out very fast. If you are caught in a rip current, do not panic – attract attention in any way you can, then float on the water to conserve your energy.

❺ Be careful if you are on a lilo or inflatable, as an offshore breeze (wind blowing from land to sea) can carry you into dangerous territory.

❻ If you are exploring the coastline on foot, ask local people for advice about the tide, watch out for safety signs and keep away from unstable ground.

THE NORTHWEST PASSAGE

The Northwest Passage is a route through the Arctic Ocean connecting the Atlantic to the Pacific. Many brave explorers have attempted the route – and not all of them made it home. This is a cruel place of sea ice, storms, and polar bears. Back in 2010, six of us set off in a Zodiac Rigid Inflatable Boat (RIB)...

▲ Our 11-m-long Shockwave Zodiac RIB was powered by three 300-horsepower engines. The aluminium hull was designed to be lightweight and tough.

▼ Big seas constantly battered our tiny craft. One giant wave jolted one of our team off his seat, whacking his head and drawing a lot of blood.

GETTING WINDY

My team planned to make it across 3,148 km of icy Arctic Ocean to raise awareness of global warming and make money for charity. On 30th August 2010, we set off from Canada's Baffin Island and wove through islands that are connected by thick ice in winter. From there, we moved into the Beaufort Sea, named after Sir Francis Beaufort, who developed the Beaufort Wind Force Scale – and we faced mighty winds here, as well as driving rain and thick mist!

DEADLY ICE

Sea ice was by far our biggest threat. Past expeditions were forced to cut their way through thick ice, but due to global warming, we could navigate around it. Sometimes, though, we had no choice but to push through the ice. If our boat struck one of these sharp pieces of floating ice, it could bring the expedition to a terrible end.

► Picking our way through the ice felt like playing a giant game of draughts... and one false move could be disastrous.

HELP FROM OUR FRIENDS

When we went ashore for the night on deserted islands, we always took shifts on bear-watch. The scent of our food could carry for miles, and the last thing we needed was a close encounter with a hungry polar bear! We were fortunate that the generous Inuit people of these far north regions supplied us with regular gasoline stops to refuel our engines. Thanks to them and our close-knit team, we finally arrived at our destination, the hamlet of Tuktoyaktuk in Canada's Northwest Territories, on 9th September. Feeling solid earth under my boots was a relief, but I would miss the wilds of the Arctic Ocean.

◄ When ashore, we kept a shotgun and a can of bear spray handy at all times.

▲ To increase our chances of success, we set out in the summer months, when average temperatures range from -10°C to +10°C.

FINDING YOUR WAY

Learning how to read maps will allow you to truly experience the world around you. Although it takes practice, there is nothing like the feeling of achievement when you reach your planned destination!

MAP CARE

As you walk, you will need to look at your map quite often to check you are on the right track. Maps need to be folded carefully to keep them in good condition so that they stay useful.

CONTOUR LINES

'Topographical' maps are often used for hiking and orienteering. They show contour lines, which are useful because they tell us how the ground is shaped. Every hiker should be able to 'read' the contour lines on the map so that they can plan their route. Each contour line on a map joins up points where the ground is the same height. Lines close together mean that there is a steep slope, while lines that are far apart indicate flat ground or a gentle slope.

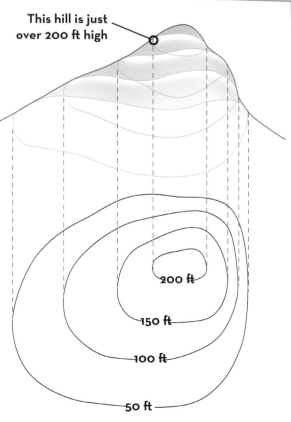

This hill is just over 200 ft high

200 ft

150 ft

100 ft

50 ft

▶ Identify useful landmarks, such as a church tower, particularly those that are on higher ground.

SYMBOLS

Maps use symbols, lines, and colours to describe what is on the land and make the map clearer. A key (or legend) explains what these symbols mean. The symbols could be pictures, words, or abbreviations. Try learning a few basic symbols so you can recognise them easily:

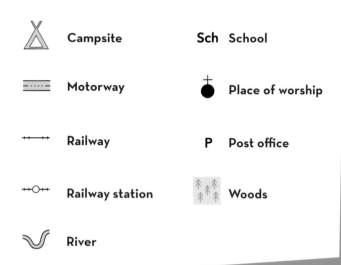

Campsite   **Sch**   School

Motorway   Place of worship

Railway   **P**   Post office

Railway station   Woods

River

SCALES

Maps are made to scale so that the distance between landmarks and places in real life is shown accurately on paper. Scale also helps us to work out distances. The scale is shown visually on a map in both centimetres and inches. In this example, this diagram shows a map with a scale of 1:100,000. In this case, every one centimetre on the map is equal to one kilometre on the ground.

▼ Use the scale to work out how long it will take to walk to your desination.

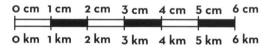

GRID REFERENCES

Maps are often divided into squares called grids. These grids help to pinpoint a location on the map quickly. The vertical lines crossing the map from top to bottom are called 'eastings' because the numbers go up as you move east across the map. The horizontal lines crossing the map from one side to the other are called 'northings' as the numbers increase as you get further north.

▶ When you give a grid reference you always give the eastings first. The forest is in 5742.

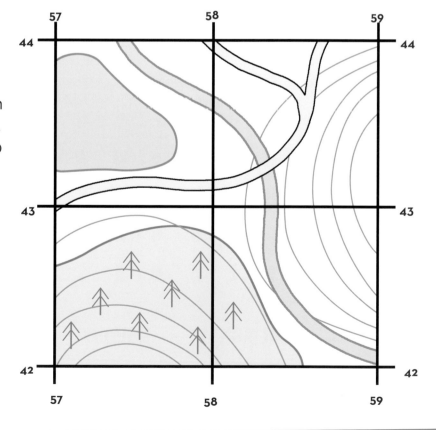

ALL AT SEA

Try out these fishy puzzles to learn a little more about what makes the underwater world so strange and spectacular. Get ready to dive in... no swimming costume required!

FISHY WORD SEARCH

Find all of these fish in the word search, and tick them off as you find them.

F	P	I	H	S	T	R	U	O	C
S	K	A	T	E	R	E	E	G	R
R	G	E	S	T	H	K	N	T	O
T	R	C	O	N	I	I	O	A	W
R	O	T	R	G	R	L	M	L	N
R	U	O	G	R	O	C	L	P	G
C	P	D	E	A	L	T	A	W	W
H	E	H	P	U	A	D	S	L	K
H	R	T	A	R	O	U	G	H	Y
A	A	H	N	C	Z	A	M	A	S

SKATE **SALMON** **ROUGHY**

HERRING **COD** **GROUPER**

OCEAN MIX-UP

Match each clue to the correct ocean.

1. This is the smallest ocean.
2. This is the biggest ocean.
3. This is 6 million km² bigger than the Arctic.
4. This is the third largest ocean.
5. This is smaller than the Pacific, but bigger than the Indian.

A. **Pacific** 162 million km²

B. **Indian** 74 million km²

C. **Atlantic** 107 million km²

D. **Arctic** 14 million km²

E. **Antarctic** 20 million km²

CURRENT CALCULATIONS

A river of water that flows through the ocean is called a current. Some currents flow very quickly.

1. Look at these currents' speeds and circle the current that is travelling the fastest.

   a) 200 cm per second
   b) 100 mm per second
   c) 1 m per second

2. How many centimetres are in a metre?

WHALE OF A TIME

Whale sharks eat tiny ocean animals, which they suck into their huge mouths. They are most common in warm oceans, where divers can swim alongside them. Can you find four differences between these two pictures of a whale shark?

GHOST SHIP

The *Flying Dutchman* was a ship that was lost at sea in a terrible storm. Some people believe that the ghost of the ship, and its crew, still sail the seas! Colour in this picture of the infamous ghost ship.

THERE ARE ABOUT 3 MILLION WRECKS IN THE OCEANS!

DANGERS IN THE DEEP

GREAT WHITE SHARKS CAN GROW OVER 6 M LONG!

Venom, spines, and strength are great ways for a predator to get lunch, or for an animal to defend itself from attacks. Marine creatures have plenty of these tricks, which is why it's always a good idea to look at sea creatures, but don't touch! In particular, keep your eyes open for these deadly creatures.

PUFFERFISH

There are lots of species of pufferfish, mostly found in tropical waters. They are usually slow, but can put on a sudden burst of speed when frightened. They also have an extremely elastic stomach, which puffs up with water (or air if taken out of water), and spiny, often poisonous skin and internal organs. This defence mechanism is designed to choke and poison a predator if they get swallowed.

BLUE-RINGED OCTOPUS

Octopuses are soft-bodied organisms with eight arms, or tentacles. Blue-ringed octopuses are around the size of a golf ball – and peaceful creatures if left alone. If disturbed, these octopuses can bite, but the bite can be so small you may not even notice. However, each animal contains enough venom in its saliva to kill 26 adults within minutes. An antidote has not yet been invented.

deflated pufferfish

inflated pufferfish

STINGRAY

These fish are related to sharks. They are mainly found in tropical and subtropical seas. Most rays have a venomous barbed stinger that is used for self-defence. Steve Irwin was a television presenter and conservationist who was known for filming dangerous animals. In 2006, he was tragically killed by a stingray while filming as a barb went through his heart.

⚠ SHARK ATTACK

The great white is responsible for more human injuries and deaths than any other shark. Despite this, it actually prefers to eat other things.

❶ If you see a shark, leave it alone. Around half of attacks could have been avoided by not interfering with the fish.

❷ Try to remain calm, but get away from a shark as fast as possible.

❸ Hit the shark in the eye or gills (not the nose) if you are trying to make it let go.

❹ Sharks can smell blood from over a mile away, so don't get in the water if you are bleeding and get out if you injure yourself.

❺ Avoid bright, flashy swimwear and jewellery as sharks are attracted to shiny things.

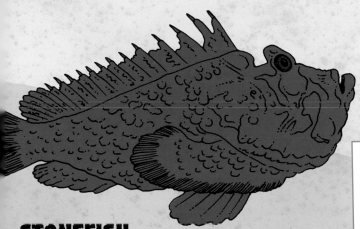

STONEFISH

Considered one of the most venomous fish, stonefish are extremely well camouflaged and often sting people in Australia when they accidentally step on them – the foot pressing down causes a sharp spine to pop up. A sting can kill, but is usually treated by putting the affected foot in hot water or administering antivenom in more serious cases.

SHARK TRUST

◀ Sharks and rays need help if they're to have a healthy future. The Shark Trust are working hard to protect sharks and you too can help. Just visit their website (https://www.sharktrust.org/), learn more about these amazing animals and see how you can get involved with shark conservation.

CONESNAIL

These large tropical sea snails have a barbed tooth that they can extend out of their heads to inject venom. Conesnails prey on small fish that live on the bottom of the ocean – but they can kill humans. They often have beautiful shells and people sometimes pick them up to look at them and get stung.

WILD WEATHER

Adventuring in all different kinds of weather can be very fun, but all weathers present their own problems. It's important to know how to predict what the weather is going to do, particularly when the sea is involved!

CLOUD WATCHING

Clouds are floating masses of moisture – either tiny water droplets or ice crystals. Different types of clouds suggest that fine weather, storms, or rain are on the way, so recognising clouds is a vital survival skill.

High cirrus clouds contain ice crystals. They do not produce rain.

Giant cumulonimbus clouds are wider at the top than bottom. They bring thunderstorms, heavy rain, and hail.

Cumulus clouds are white and puffy. If they stay white, it will not rain. If they turn grey, it means the water droplets in the clouds are getting big and heavy – and it will soon rain!

Low, grey stratus clouds bring rain or snow.

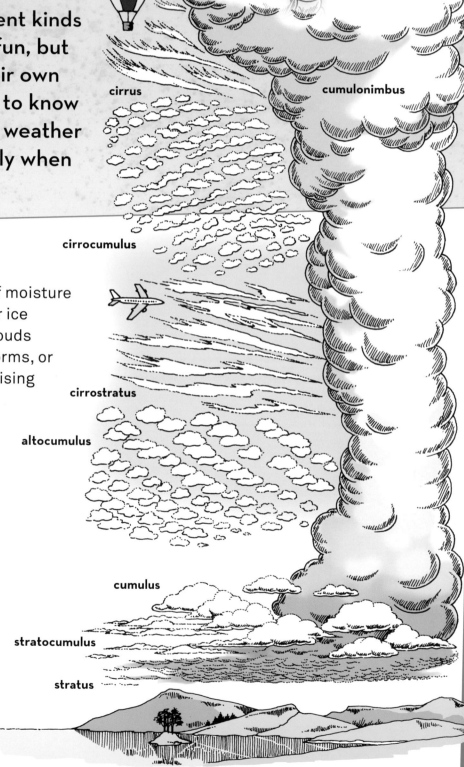

cirrus

cumulonimbus

cirrocumulus

cirrostratus

altocumulus

cumulus

stratocumulus

stratus

COASTAL WEATHER

Coasts generally have a mild and rainy climate. But keep your eye on the weather at the coast, as it can blow up breezy pretty fast!

Coastal fog

Fog often forms off coasts where warm, moist air makes contact with the cold water surface. The water in the air condenses into low clouds. Thick fog makes it harder for ships to detect hazards such as rocks.

High winds

Coasts are generally breezy places because of on- and offshore winds. The strongest winds usually blow in off the sea.

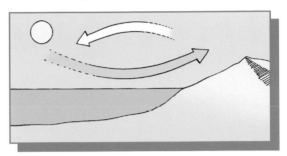

▲ **Onshore breeze: by day, warm air rises off the land and is replaced by cooler air blowing off the sea.**

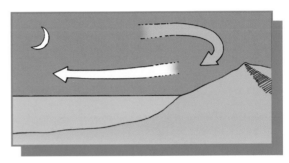

▲ **Offshore breeze: at night, cool air sinks over the land and moves out to sea to replace warm air that is rising from the water.**

Hurricanes

Tropical coasts are at risk of hurricanes. Hurricanes form over warm oceans in hot, sticky weather. As a group of thunderstorms combine, warm, moist air shoots upwards and starts to spiral. If these whirling storms blow ashore, they can wreck buildings and drive boats onto land. High seas caused by storm surges can produce floods.

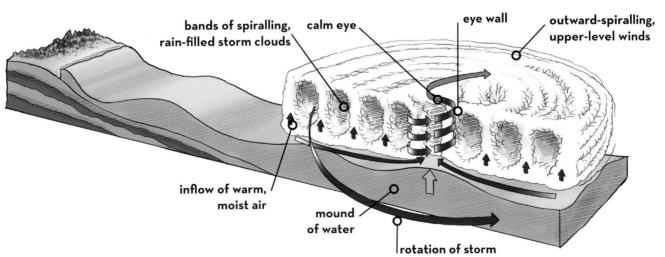

bands of spiralling, rain-filled storm clouds

calm eye

eye wall

outward-spiralling, upper-level winds

inflow of warm, moist air

mound of water

rotation of storm

FUN FACTS

TALLEST MOUNTAIN

Although Mount Everest is the world's highest mountain, the tallest mountain is the volcano Mauna Kea, in Hawaii. It is over 10,000 m tall, although less than half of it (4,207 m) is above sea level – the rest is under the Pacific Ocean.

MOST VENOMOUS SPIDER

The Brazilian wandering spider, which is found mainly in tropical South America, is considered the world's most venomous spider. During the day, it hides in dark places such as clothes, cars, boots, and boxes, where it may bite if accidentally disturbed.

BIGGEST FLOWER

The biggest flower in the world is the corpse flower, which can grow up to 1 m in diameter. It smells like rotting flesh in order to attract flies which then help it pollinate.

LARGEST BIRD

The largest bird is the ostrich, which lives on the plains of Africa and Arabia. A male ostrich can reach a height of 2.8 m and weigh over 156 kg.

DEADLIEST PLANT

Tobacco use causes more than 5 million deaths every year, making it the most deadly plant in the world. All parts of the plant contain the toxic substances nicotine and anabasine. Dried tobacco leaves are mainly used for smoking. People who smoke are far more likely to suffer diseases such as cancer than people who don't smoke.

HOTTEST PLACE

The highest temperature ever recorded was 56.7°C. It was measured in Death Valley, in the western United States, in July 1913.

LONGEST MIGRATION

Arctic terns are amazing birds that breed in the Arctic, then fly to Antarctica. They have been recorded flying nearly 90,000 km per year – the longest migration of any animal in the world!

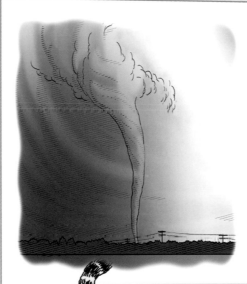

FASTEST WIND

The fastest winds on Earth blow inside tornadoes. The fastest speed ever clocked was 486 km/h, in a tornado that hit Oklahoma City, in the United States, in 1999.

FASTEST LAND ANIMAL

The fastest animal on land is the cheetah, which has been recorded at speeds of 109–120 km/h. It can accelerate from 0–96 km/h in three seconds.

GLOSSARY

Altitude – The height above sea level.

Asthma – A condition that causes difficulty with breathing.

Avalanche – A mass of snow, ice, or rocks falling down a mountainside.

Barb – A sharp point or bristle.

Cache – A hidden food store.

Cardio Pulmonary Resuscitation (CPR) – A life-saving procedure carried out when somebody's breathing or heart has stopped.

Climate – The regular pattern of weather experienced in a region over many years.

Clotting – When a liquid thickens so that it can no longer flow.

Cloud – A mass of tiny water droplets or ice crystals floating in the air.

Cocoon – A protective case made by an animal.

Condensation – When a gas changes into a liquid, as when invisible water vapour changes into water.

Constellation – A group of stars that seem to form a pattern in the night sky.

Crevasse – A deep, open crack in ice or rock.

Current – The movement of a stream of water in an ocean or river.

Deforestation – The cutting down of trees in a large area.

Dehydration – When the body lacks water.

Desert – An area where less than 25 cm of rain or snow falls in a year.

Drought – A long period with less than normal rainfall.

Edible – Something that can be eaten.

Ember – A glowing spark.

Equator – An imaginary line around the Earth's middle.

Evaporation – When a liquid, such as water, changes into a gas.

Evolve – To change gradually, usually over thousands of years.

Faeces - Poo.

Frostbite - Injury to the body caused by extreme cold.

Fungi - The group of living things that includes mushrooms and toadstools.

Habitat - The natural environment of a living thing.

Hibernation - When an animal spends the winter resting.

Humid - When the air contains a high amount of moisture.

Hypothermia - When the body loses heat in cold temperatures.

Insulator - A substance, such as trapped air, that does not easily let heat pass through.

Invertebrate - An animal without a backbone, such as an insect, crab or octopus.

Mammal - An animal that has a backbone and hair or fur. Females usually give birth to live young, which they feed with milk.

Navigation - Finding your position and following a route.

Paralyse - To make a person or animal become unable to move.

Predator - An animal that hunts and kills other animals for food.

Prey - An animal that is hunted and killed for food.

Protein - A nutrient found in foods such as meat, fish, milk, eggs, nuts and beans, that allows the body to work.

Rainforest - A thick forest, usually found in tropical areas with high rainfall.

Species - A group of living things that look similar and can breed together.

Subtropical - In a region just to the north or south of the tropics, where the weather does not usually get very cold.

Tide - The rising and falling of the sea, which usually happens twice a day on any particular beach.

Topographical - A topographical map shows the shape of the ground (e.g. flat or hilly) using contour lines.

Tropical - In a region close to the Equator, where the weather is hot all year round.

Unconscious - Not awake and aware of what is happening.

Urine - Pee.

Vegetation - Plants.

Venom - A poisonous substance produced by an animal.

ANSWERS

Page 14
Dot to dot

Page 15
Make a word
HABITAT

Page 22
Problem solver
1,200,000 km²

Page 23
Identify the animal
1. GOLDEN LION TAMARIN   2. RUFFED LEMUR
3. SUMATRAN RHINO   4. HELMETED HORNBILL
5. QUEEN ALEXANDRA'S BIRDWING

Page 38
Finding north

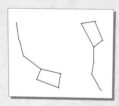

Scrambled animals
1. SEAL   2. PENGUIN
3. MUSK OXEN   4. POLAR BEAR
5. ORCA   6. WALRUS

Page 39
Survival strategies
1. **POLAR BEAR:**
   I have massive claws that help me catch seals.
2. **SEAL:**
   I spend a lot of time underwater hiding from polar bears.
3. **WALRUS:**
   I am very fat and have long whiskers and two long tusks.
4. **ARCTIC FOX:**
   I have a bushy tail that I wrap around my body for warmth.
5. **MUSK OXEN:**
   I have layers of thick shaggy fur and horns on my head.

Polar night and day
The season would be summer.
There are 6 hours of darkness.

Page 52
Meerkat madness

Secret animal
GROUND SQUIRREL

Page 53
Camel discoverer
1. Asia   2. Bactrian
3. 16   4. Dromedary

Page 62
Fishy word search

Ocean mix-up
1. Arctic   2. Pacific
3. Antarctic   4. Indian
5. Atlantic

Current calculations
1. A
2. 100

Page 63
Whale of a time